YOUR KNOWLEDGE H

- We will publish your bachelor's and master's thesis, essays and papers

- Your own eBook and book - sold worldwide in all relevant shops

- Earn money with each sale

Upload your text at www.GRIN.com
and publish for free

Conversion Therapy in "The Miseducation of Cameron Post" by Emily M. Danforth

Tabea Wiegand

Bibliographic information published by the German National Library:

The German National Library lists this publication in the National Bibliography; detailed bibliographic data are available on the Internet at http://dnb.dnb.de.

ISBN: 9783346613240
This book is also available as an ebook.

© GRIN Publishing GmbH
Nymphenburger Straße 86
80636 München

Print and binding: Books on Demand GmbH, Norderstedt, Germany
Printed on acid-free paper from responsible sources.

The present work has been carefully prepared. Nevertheless, authors and publishers do not incur liability for the correctness of information, notes, links and advice as well as any printing errors.

GRIN web shop: https://www.grin.com/document/1184326

Rheinische Friedrich-Wilhelms-Universität Bonn

Institut für Anglistik, Amerikanistik und Keltologie

The Portrayal of Conversion Therapy in *The Miseducation of Cameron Post*

Term Paper for/Hausarbeit für

Queer Rights in the USA: What's Next After Marriage Equality?

Summer Term/Sommersemester 2021

Hennef, den 14.10.2021

Table of contents

Introduction

Throughout history, the opinion regarding members of the LGBTQ+-community has changed drastically. From accepting homosexuality[1] as normal in ancient Greece (cf. Mondimore 4ff.) to presenting homosexuality as a sin in medieval and still modern times. Nowadays an overall accepting and even supporting position for the community can be seen, but certain negative tendencies still exist.

Those negative tendencies can be especially seen in the church and are often validated with religious arguments but naturally, not all tendencies can be noticed from religious institutions. Those tendencies differ in intensity; however, a certain number of individuals is feeling threatened by members of the LGBTQ+-community and desire to interfere in personal lives to change the homosexuality of a person. This is often done with conversion therapy.

Conversion therapy is an issue that many people are unaware of but if they do know of it, people are commonly uncertain of what conversion therapy is like. Most information is gathered from media and books as in the book *The Miseducation of Cameron Post*. The teenage girl Cameron Post is sent to a conversion therapy camp to be cured of her homosexuality. Before and during her time in the camp, she writes down her experiences and her eventual escape.

Since conversion therapy is not banned in all US states and considering that society only knows about conversion therapy through books and media, it is interesting to examine if the conversion therapy in *The Miseducation of Cameron Post* is an accurate portrayal of conversion therapy in the United States in the 1990s.

To understand conversion therapy, the different forms of conversion therapy will be elaborated, and the methods, treatment, and effects will be detailed. Since the primary source is a young adult[2] novel, it is additionally important to look at features of YA fiction and especially of YA protagonists. In the next step, the young adult novel *The Miseducation of Cameron Post* will be analyzed regarding the attitude of the protagonist before attending conversion camp and her time during her stay.

---

[1] It is understood that not all survivors of conversion therapy are homosexual but also e.g., bisexual. For simplification not all sexual orientations will be listed but only homosexuality. Nevertheless, all sexual orientations are considered.
[2] Will be shortened to YA in the following

Furthermore, the methods, the effects, and the main counselor will be analyzed, concerning the theoretical section.

Regarding the listed method of this term paper, it will be determined that *The Miseducation of Cameron Post* is an inaccurate portrayal of conversion therapy in special regards to the protagonist with tendencies to an accurate portrayal. The reason for the inaccurate portrayal is mainly due to the protagonist being a YA protagonist and hence diminishing the survivor's experiences.

1. Defining an accurate image of conversion therapy in the United States in the 1990s

The following chapter will focus on different forms of conversion therapy and the methods. Furthermore, it will be looked at the effects of conversion therapy.

1.1. Health care and religious conversion therapy

To understand conversion therapy and the substance of *The Miseducation of Cameron Post*, it is important to look at the different forms of conversion therapy and its methods of therapy to create an image of conversion therapy in the United States in the 1990s.

Conversion therapy is practiced by either "licensed professionals in the context of providing health care and by some clergy or other spiritual advisors in the context of religious practice" (Mallory, et al. 1). Although conversion therapy by health care does exist, there is a significantly greater number of LGBTQ+ youth being in conversion therapy by religious or spiritual institutions (cf. ibid.). Out of 83,000 thousand young LGBTQ+ young adults (age 13-17) across all states of the US, 57,000 were sent to conversion therapy by a religious or spiritual institution (cf. ibid.)[3]. There is a difference between two types of conversion therapy and both therapies have different approaches and methods of therapy, but since this term paper and the primary literature will only address religious conversion therapy, health care conversion therapy will not be analyzed further.

Conversion therapy is hence practiced more by religious institutions than by health care institutions.

---

[3] Although this survey is dated in 2018, no major change in those numbers could be found for the last three years.

1.2. Methods of therapy and treatment in the 1990s in the US

In the 1990s, different methods were introduced to cure homosexuals of their sexuality. There are two approaches of treatment, that can be distinguished by, while one focuses more on invasive methods and the other more on an emotional and cognitive level. By invasive, the following methods by Douglas C. Haldemann were indicated:

These include[d] psychoanalytic therapy, prayer and spiritual interventions, electric shock, nausea-inducing drugs, hormone therapy, surgery, turbatory reconditioning, rest, visits to prostitutes, and excessive bicycle riding. (221)

This clearly illustrates how all listed methods are intrusive and hurting the individuals and trying to cure homosexuality by forcing feelings and thoughts out of the individual's[4] mind. Those and more intrusive methods were also listed by Tozer and McClanahan that also included visits to prostitutes and enhancing relationships with the other gender by isolating the individual with a person of the other gender for two weeks (723).

Apart from the invasive methods, the cognition-focused methods are less intrusive and less harmful for the body of the patient. Those methods are still mentally abusive to the individual but less harmful for the body in the moment of treatment and therefore less invasive and harmful. The "cognitive-behavioral therapy [lists] recording thoughts and behaviors, changing self-talk, and distracting or reframing sexual feelings," (Beckstead, Morrow 664). The individual's mentality and thought process is tried to be changed but not by force but rather by manipulation of making the individual realize that their feelings and thoughts are not acceptable.

While the methods are clear, it is important to look at what conversion therapists[5] want to treat within the individual. First, therapists do not desire to treat the distress experienced while being in a non-accepting environment and hence feeling self-hatred about oneself (cf. Beckstead, Morrow 671).

Many conversion therapists connect their ideas to Sigmund Freud, a psychoanalyst who studied children's behavior and how parents may change sexual development through their education. In *Letter to an American mother*, Freud writes about homosexuality but apart from conversion therapists, Freud does not illustrate homosexuality as an illness, but as an "arrest of sexual development" (Freud 786.).

---

[4] Throughout this term paper the commonly used term "patient" will not be written. "Patient" implies an illness which is wrong in this context. Thus, the terms "individual" or "survivor" will be used in the term paper.
[5] In the context of this term paper the term "therapist" will be used. A conversion therapist mustn't be compared to a professional and licensed therapist but out of simplification, the term will be used in the term paper.

Freud is not a defender of homosexuality, but conversion therapists are basing their arguments on a person who would not agree with their therapeutic approach.

There is a difference between intrusive and cognition-focused methods that are physically and mentally abusive. Furthermore, conversion therapists are not treating the individual's distress and are building their theory on Sigmund Freud who would disagree with their opinion.

1.3. Effects of Conversion therapy

When talking about Conversion therapy, most only consider the negative aspects of homosexuals being mentally and physically tortured for their sexuality. While this is indeed true, many survivors share a more positive feeling of being understood for the first time and not being alone with their feelings at the beginning of conversion therapy. (cf. Beckstead, Morrow 668-669). Furthermore, patients experienced relief from knowing of an institution that may help them with their homosexuality, as most were not self-accepting of that (cf. ibid.; cf. Nicolosi 150). That is also the reason why most survivors went to Conversion therapy voluntarily - after having consulted with a trustworthy religious figure in their church – to have someone help with their self-hatred and distress (cf. ibid. 666-667).

Besides those first positive feelings about Conversion therapy, survivors suffer from decreased same-sex attraction due to having had to suppress their feelings before and especially during conversion therapy (cf. Beckstead, Morrow 680). Apart from that, survivors suffer from "increased guilt, anxiety, and low self-esteem." (Haldemann 225) for not being able to be cured from conversion therapy. Furthermore, survivors may suffer from increased substance abuse, are more suicidal, and feel untrue with themselves (cf. Glassgold et al. 50). Moreover, the relationship between the survivors and individuals in their life (e.g., parents, LGBTQ+-friends, romantic partners) suffers due to the therapy, since the as unnatural seen sexuality is usually blamed on the people in the survivor's life (cf. ibid.).

Apart from the first positive feeling, conversion therapy survivors suffer from a great number of mental issues after having had to go to conversion therapy.

2.0. Defining Young Adult fiction and its protagonists

YA fiction is defined by having a story about "school-aged characters" (Williams 2014). In the 21st century, literature experienced a drastic change in YA fiction in regards to the variety of topics and themes that would have not been written about a

4

few years ago (cf. Kaplan 11). This change can be explained by authors wanting to reach a broader audience and in virtue of the perspective of young adults today (cf. ibid. 11,18). As a result of social media and being connected to diversity all over the world, young adults are more in contact with dissimilar cultures, etc., and are therefore more in need of reading novels about alternative dynamics (cf. ibid.).

The protagonists in YA fiction are quite different from adult fiction. Most YA protagonists suffer from trauma or are experiencing mental and emotional challenges but will eventually overcome those and develop to a better version of themselves (cf. Williams 2014). Furthermore, especially female protagonists are considered as "heroines" who are and feel differently from their social environment (cf. ibid). While this can, on one hand, create a well-written and diverse character, this can on the other hand lead to a problem YA novels often obtain. By wanting to have a tremendous different and multifarious protagonist, the plot and topic of the novel are obstructed and can be portrayed falsely (cf. Roxburgh 6).

YA novels are written for young adults who want diverse literature. Furthermore, the protagonists are complex and stand out, which can however lead to an overshadowing of the theme of the novel.

3.0. The portrayal of conversion therapy in "The Miseducation of Cameron Post"

The succeeding chapters will focus on the portrayal of conversion therapy in the novel *The Miseducation of Cameron Post*. To analyze the portrayal in the mentioned book, the main protagonist will be analyzed regarding her portrayal as a young teenager who is involuntarily sent to a conversion camp. Moreover, the methods, effects, and supervisors of the camp will be analyzed.

To understand certain thoughts of this term paper, it is important to give a summary of certain aspects of the book. When Cameron was still a young child, her parents died during a weekend trip that Cameron was not part of (cf. Danforth 23-25). Since then, she grew up with her grandmother and her Aunt Ruth and (cf. ibid. 25-28) and later with Ruth's boyfriend called Ray (cf. ibid. 108).

3.1. Cameron right before going to Conversion therapy

After the local Pastor and her family found out about her relationship with the girl Coley, they immediately decided to send Cameron to the conversion camp *God's Promise* (cf. Danforth 246). Cameron was shocked by them finding out as she

5

repeatedly said "Coley told, Coley told, Coley told. And then: They know, they know, they know." (Danforth 248). While Cameron's reaction to her family finding out about her relationship with Coley may be reasonable, it is also an accurate reaction of young adult conversion therapy survivors. While most adult survivors went to conversion therapy voluntarily (cf. Beckstead, Morrow 666f.), adolescents are still more likely to be sent to residential conversion therapy by their parents without their children's consent (cf. Glassgold et al. 72). A survivor of conversion therapy also described the additive isolation from friends and family (cf. Calhoun 2018), which is simply traumatizing for young adults. Cameron's initial reaction is hence accurate and helps create a realistic image of conversion therapy.

While Cameron's reaction is realistic, during the drive to *God's Promise,* it can already be seen that Cameron Post's attitude towards conversion therapy is different from her finding out and from studies and reports[6] of survivors. Instead of feeling relieved for finally finding a place that may help her, she is opposing it. This can be seen by the dialogue between Cameron and her aunt Ruth who is driving her to the camp. Ruth tells Cameron how she must be open for the camp and that "[she] can't understand why anyone would want to stay like this if they knew they could change" (Danforth 264). Cameron answers with irony and jokes about Ruth's comments and apart from that, both stay silent. Cameron also calls the conversion camp a "fucked-up place" (Danforth 282) which shows how Cameron is not open and convinced about the effectiveness of the camp. Furthermore, Cameron thinks that her aunt's and grandma's worries about her going to conversion therapy are not justified. After Ruth dropped Cameron off at the camp and says her goodbyes, Cameron snaps and blames Ruth for her homosexuality. Cameron knows that she is lying (cf. Danforth 283) but after she made Ruth cry, Cameron feels "that, finally, finally, I had actually done something awful enough to deserve that reaction" (ibid.). By that Cameron states that her homosexuality does not deserve the reaction she received regarding it and how for her, being homosexual is not a valid reason for crying.

Cameron's different attitude towards conversion therapy is also noticeable by her labeling herself. Beckstead and Morrow analyzed that survivors of conversion therapy do not label themselves as LGBTQ+ but were in refusal of that or adapted labels (e.g.

---

[6] It is known that self-reports can be misleading sources. To secure legitimacy, only credible self-reports were included or those of professional studies.

pervert) that their social environment gave them (664-665). On the car ride to the camp, Ruth buys Cameron a can of sour cream and onion Pringles that Cameron rejects with the explanation that "all lesbians [hate] [it]." (Danforth 259) Cameron also labels others, as the children at *God's Promise* who she names "homos" but not in an offending meaning but rather jokingly (Danforth, 271).

While this is not typical behavior it can be explained with Cameron's friend Lindsey. Lindsey is an open lesbian who does not live in Cameron's hometown (Miles City) but who Cameron met during the summer break at a swimming contest. Both spent the summer before Cameron was sent to conversion therapy together and Cameron explored her sexuality with Lindsey (cf. Danforth 96f.). Furthermore, Cameron had a flirtatious relationship with one of her lifeguard co-workers – Mona Harris – with whom she could also explore her sexuality (cf. ibid. 239ff.). Thus, Cameron has been unlike most survivors of conversion therapy (cf. Beckstead, Morrow 662) in contact with the LGBTQ+-community before going to *God's Promise*, which explains her skeptical attitude towards conversion therapy. While Cameron's skepticism is clear and understandable, the accurateness of Cameron's attitude is doubtable which leads to an untrue portrayal of conversion therapy survivors and therefore diminishes their experiences.

Although Cameron's social environment is quite religious, Cameron is only influenced by that to an extend. She feels uncomfortable in church as "[her] face [was] hot and [her] skin itchy," (Danforth 99). Cameron is in addition to that skeptical if any God exists (cf. ibid. 100) which shows her not conforming to her social environment and therefore representing the protagonist of a young adult novel. But hence Cameron does spend most of her free time in church, she is nevertheless slightly influenced in her vocabulary and way of thinking. Cameron goes with her aunt to church every Sunday and Ruth also made her join the church's youth group "Firepower" (ibid. 67). When sitting in church, Cameron felt "like [she] should at least be attempting to save [her]self, even if it was halfhearted," (ibid.). Sentences as "saving myself" and feeling like she must save herself show the influence her church had on her. Moreover, Cameron does call Lindsey "the pervert" (ibid.) and refers to homosexuality as "sin" (ibid.) and therefore has adopted the vocabulary of her homophobic church. Although Cameron is in an environment that should influence her thinking of sexuality grandly (Haldemann, Gay Rights, Patient Rights 262) and still does, Cameron views her

7

homosexuality as normal, and although she calls Lindsey "the pervert" (Danforth 100), she does not see Lindsey as the reason for her sexual orientation. Cameron is aware that she was not influenced by Lindsey but acts of her own will, as she says: "How could I pretend to be a victim when I was so willing to sin?" (ibid.). This is unusual thinking as many LGBTQ+ young adults in the 1990s were convinced that their religious environment and their beliefs are more important than the individual sexual identity (cf. Beckstead, Morrow 663). Cameron believing her sexuality is valid and more important than religion is hence an inaccurate portrayal and only enhances a false image for the readers.

Cameron Post is portrayed as skeptical and as if she is taking the situation not seriously. As a survivor of Conversion therapy said, the skepticism and joking behavior of Cameron Post is not accurate to the feelings of young adults who are sent to conversion therapy (cf. Silman 2018). While the rather rebellious behavior fits a protagonist of a YA novel, the portrayal of a character in the 1990s in the US who is sent to conversion therapy is inaccurate. Even though a non-conforming character is more interesting to read, this diminishes conversion therapy survivors, as Roxbourgh similarly noted in his analysis regarding YA novels (cf. 6). Conversion therapy is a topic that many people have heard of but rarely know about and by having an inaccurate protagonist, a false image is spread that contributes to untrue preconceptions. Furthermore, survivors who were not skeptical of conversion therapy are pictured as weak and dense.

3.2. The Methods of *God's Promise*

The methods of *God's Promise* are non-invasive and focus on cognitive therapy. At the beginning of therapy, the children of the camp must do weekly one-on-one sessions with their counselors and bible studies (cf. Danforth 269, 297). After having been in the program long enough, the children join weekly group support sessions (cf. ibid. 357).

Regarding their stay in the camp, arrivers are not granted privileges to decorate their room but only after having stayed three months in camp and having made the impression of making process (cf. ibid. 273, 291). Furthermore, the children are not allowed to have contact with their families and are not granted the privilege to receive personal mail and gifts until their supervisors feel they are ready for that (cf. ibid.

330). Adding to the previous point, the supervisors always must approve the decoration item (cf. ibid. 357). Hence, the camp can control the children's influences.

God's Promise is like most conversion therapy institutions focusing on gender conformity. Beckstead and Morrow discovered that wanting to enhance the gender the individual was born with, is one of the important aspects of conversion therapy (667). *God's Promise* is doing that, by having the children do "gender-appropriate activity" (Danforth 298), besides their daily chores and school (cf. ibid. 297ff.). For boys, this includes outdoor activities and sport that enhances strength, while the girls go on shopping and beauty salon trips and improve skills a future housewife would need (cf. ibid. 299f.). Furthermore, Cameron is not supposed to be called "Cam" anymore, since it is "an even more masculine adaption of [her] already androgynous name." (ibid. 382). The problem herewith is that defining sexuality regarding behavior and gender identity is tremendously damaging for the development of young adults (cf. Haldemann 221). Since Danforth is addressing the topic in her novel, she is emphasizing the experience of survivors and creating an accurate image of conversion therapy.

Apart from those activities, the camp focuses on strengthening the religious belief of the children by having spiritual sessions that include "prayer/devotional hours" and trips to the nearby church in Bozeman (ibid.). By strengthening the religious belief and relationship to God, the Camp guarantees "people [to] escape these kinds of unwanted desires" (ibid. 207). Religious conversion therapy is grandly focusing on the individual's religious belief hence thinking that homosexuality can be cured by intensifying spiritual thinking (Beckstead, Morrow 665, 667; Haldemann 221, 224).

3.2.1. The Iceberg Metaphor

During Cameron's first one-on-one session, she is introduced to the method of creating a personal iceberg for every individual at *God's Promise*. The goal of this method is for young adults to find the reason that led to their homosexuality. The tip of the iceberg represents homosexuality and a ship sailing towards the iceberg the social environment. The important point of this metaphor is that:

> The sin of homosexual desire and behavior is so scary and imposing that they [social environment] become fixed on it, consumed and horrified by it, when in actuality, the big problems, the problems we need to deal with, they're hidden away below the surface. (Danforth 288)

9

The counselors are thus not focusing on the distress of conflicting with their homosexuality but rather on the past experiences and thereby treating the homosexuality, as Beckstead and Morrow analyzed with survivors (cf. 671). Therefore, survivors cannot feel mentally better which leads to an unsuccessful process in conversion therapy and will result in "increased guilt, anxiety, and low self-esteem" (cf. Haldemann 225) for not having succeeded in therapy.

The iceberg metaphor is commonly used by therapists as a survivor mentioned this in an interview (cf. Silman 2018). The interview focused on survivors' opinions regarding *The Miseducation of Cameron Post* and the interviewed mentioned how Cameron's reaction to the metaphor was different from theirs. They felt relieved and hoped for having found a method that would make them understand their sexuality and the included mental distress better. Cameron on the other hand feels different about the metaphor and tells Rick memories from her past that convey the impression as if Cameron is voluntarily trying to change her homosexuality, while Cameron is just conforming to the program. Survivors of conversion therapy state that they started lying to their therapists about their feelings and thoughts after having had numerous sessions that turned out to be unsuccessful (cf. Silman 2018). The difference is that Cameron lies from the first session about her feelings and thoughts and realizes that "[she] hadn't come to Promise with a "teachable heart","(Danforth 295). Once again, Cameron is portrayed inaccurately as a young adult who is forced to go to a conversion camp, which contributes to the false image that survivors must have had doubts about the therapy.

As mentioned before, one aspect *God's Promise* is focusing on is gender nonconformity. All young adults at the camp have written in their iceberg elements, which include them having had "inappropriate gender modeling" (Danforth 292). An example for that would be Cameron's roommate – Viking Erin (cf. ibid.) - who had "too much masculine bonding with [her] dad over Minnesota Vikings football." (ibid.). While the camp sees gender nonconformity in childhood as the reason for homosexuality, Glassgold et al. found out that "there is no research evidence that childhood gender nonconformity and adult homosexuality are identical or necessary sequential development phenomena." (73).

3.3. Reverend Rick

Reverend Rick Roneous is first introduced to Cameron before she even got to *God's Promise* during a visit of Rick in Miles City (cf. Danforth 205). During his visit there, Rick revealed to the youth group Firepower that "[he] was a teenager who struggled with homosexual desire," (ibid. 208) but after strengthening his religious belief, he can call himself an "ex-gay" (ibid. 448). An "ex-gay" is a term frequently used in conversion therapy for people whose homosexuality was cured due to conversion therapy and who label themselves as heterosexual now (cf. Beckstead, Morrow 651). Danforth is therefore using accurate terms and thus creating an accurate image.

3.4. The Effects of *God's Promise* on the young adults

Conversion therapy has enormous long-term negative effects on individuals that are as well addressed in *The Miseducation of Cameron Post*. One aspect is the mental health of the children during their time in the camp. Cameron and the other children experience not feeling as living in their own body anymore and feeling isolated and as a stranger to themselves (cf. Danforth 312f.). Survivors experience those feelings as well (cf. Beckstead, Morrow 652) which enhances the accuracy of the children's and therefore survivor's experiences.

Studies about conversion therapy have shown that the therapy has a massive influence on the survivor's thought process. Cameron experiences that after having been in the camp for months, during the night after having thought about intimacy with women.

> But then I might hear Lydia's voice saying, *You have to fight these sinful impulses: fight, it's not supposed to be easy to fight sin,* and I might totally ignore it, or even laugh to myself about what an idiot she was, but there it would be, her voice, in my head, where it hadn't been before. And it was other stuff too, these bits and pieces of doctrine, of scripture, of life lessons here and there, until more and more of them were coated on, along for the ride, and I didn't consistently question where they had come from, or why they were there, but I did start to feel kind of weighed down by them (Danforth 361).

The given excerpt displays the isolation that the young adults are forced into that leads even involuntarily to a complete surrender to the conversion therapy (cf. Tozer, McClanahan 723; cf. Beckstead, Morrow 652) Due to the constant infiltration of conversion therapy, young adults are starting to think like their therapists, which leads to shame for their feelings and eventually to unhealthily decreased sexual attraction (cf. Beckstead, Morrow 680).

Mark Turner is a young adult of *God's Promise* who is seen as the ideal patient for conversion therapy. Besides his father being a preacher (cf. Danforth 364), he is allowed to telephone donors for money (cf. Danforth 314) and is therefore supposed to be cured within a short time.

After having been in *God's Promise* for more than a half year, Cameron experiences in a group session Mark breaking down. Mark received a letter from his father, explaining that "[he] [is] still very feminine and weak. "(Danforth 366) and how "[his father] cannot have this weakness in [his] home." (ibid.). Due to this rejection and Mark not being able to change his sexuality (cf. ibid. 369), Mark feels guilty as survivors of conversion therapy felt during and after their therapy (cf. Haldemann 224). After having talked about his father's letter, Mark does extensive sports exercises (cf. Danforth, 367ff.) to show that he is not weak but after a few moments, he breaks down crying on the floor (cf. ibid).

He is sent to his room where the supervisors are reassuring him but nevertheless, he is still in shock (cf. ibid. 370). During the night after his breakdown, Mark attempted suicide by "[using] a razor to cut his genitals several times; then he poured bleach over the wounds." (ibid. 379). By cutting his genitals, Mark symbolized wanting to get rid of any sexual attraction to be able to complete conversion therapy and be the son, his father wants to have. Many survivors, who are desperate to change their sexuality but naturally cannot, attempt suicide to not feel guilty and disappointed with themselves anymore (cf. Haldemann 225).

As a consequence of Mark's suicide attempt, inspectors from the state came to the camp to investigate if abuse is occurring in *God's Promise* (cf. Danforth 396). During their visit, Cameron decides to communicate to one inspector the emotional abuse of the camp (ibid. 397ff.). Cameron is explaining the problem of conversion therapy, that a lot of children in the camp cannot and do not even desire to change their sexuality and feel mentally abused by that (ibid. 400). Furthermore, Cameron elaborates that the children who are committing to the therapy still cannot change their sexuality and therefore blame themselves for that (ibid.). Cameron's elaboration is accurate since Psychologists as Haldemann wrote almost identical affirmations in their reports (cf. 225). Nevertheless, this shows once again the inaccurateness of Cameron being a young adult in conversion therapy. Her realizing the enormous negative effects of conversion therapy does not accord to self-reports of conversion therapy survivors (cf, Silman 2018) and consequently minimizes the experiences of survivors. While overcoming personal trauma may be fitting for a YA protagonist (cf. Williams, 2014), it is obstructing the topic of the story as Roxburgh noticed in several YA novels (cf. 6).

Conclusion

This paper has illustrated how *The Miseducation of Cameron Post* is an inaccurate portrayal of conversion therapy in the 1990s in the United States due to having an inaccurate portrayal of the main character as a teenager who is being sent to conversion therapy. Cameron is the protagonist of young adult fiction and hence is a rather rebellious character who is not conforming to her social environment. While Cameron may be a great role model for fighting conversion therapy, her disorderly behavior creates a false image of conversion therapy survivors. Cameron is accepting her sexual identity and has been confident and unquestionable about that since a young age. Moreover, Cameron is surrounded by religious institutions but does not have a connection to the church and religion in any way. Survivors of conversion therapy report a different image of themselves and are not relating to Cameron as a character. For all those reasons, the protagonist Cameron portrays a serious false image of survivors.

While Cameron is an inaccurate characterization of a teenager being sent to a conversion camp, *God's Promise* is accurately portrayed as a conversion camp. The camp forces children to their camp and is focusing on gender conformity and religious studies. Also, the effects of *God's Promise* and their abuse are being portrayed accurately and the methods are equivalent to reports of survivors. The effects of the therapy are also shown to an intense but truthful extend and show the abomination of conversion therapy.

Although the camp is an accurate portrayal, we are experiencing the camp out of Cameron's perspective and therefore, the portrayal is still inaccurate. *The Miseducation of Cameron Post* is an important part of LGBTQ+-literature and has spread awareness to the topic of conversion therapy. However, it must be read with cautiousness since it cannot be stated as an accurate portrayal of conversion therapy in the 1990s in the United States due to the overshadowing of the theme by a YA main protagonist.

Bibliography

Beckstead, A. Lee, and Susan L. "Morrow. Mormon Client's Experiences of Conversion Therapy. The Need for a New Treatment Approach." *The counseling psychologist*, vol. 32, no. 5, August 2004, pp. 651-690.

Calhoun, Dareen. "How I survived "Ex-Gay" Conversion Therapy" *Colorlines*, 14. June 2018, https://www.colorlines.com/articles/how-i-survived-ex-gay-conversion-therapy. Accessed July 16th, 2021.

Danforth, Emily. *The Miseducation of Cameron Post*, HarperCollins Publisher, 2012.

Freud, Sigmund. "Letter to an American Mother." *American Journal of Psychiatry*, vol.107 no.10, 1951, pp. 786-787.

Glassgold, Judith M., et al. *Report of the Task Force on Appropriate Therapeutic Responses to Sexual Orientation,* American Psychological Association, 2009.

Haldemann, Douglas C. "The Practice and Ethics of Sexual Orientation Conversion Therapy." *Journal of Consulting and Clinical Psychology*, vol. 62, no. 2, 1994, pp. 221-227.

---. "Gay Rights, Patient Rights. The Implications of Sexual Orientation Conversion Therapy." *Professional Psychology: Research and Practice*, vol. 33, no. 3, June 2002, pp. 260-264.

Kaplan, Jeffrey S. "Young Adult Literature in the 21st Century. Moving Beyond Traditional Constraints and Conventions." *The Alan Review*, vol. 32, no. 2, Winter 2005, pp. 11-18.

Mallory, Christy, et al. *Conversion Therapy and LGBT Youth*. The Williams Institute, 2018.

Mondimore, Francis Mark. *A natural history of homosexuality*. The Johns Hopkins University Press, 1996.

Nicolosi, Joseph. *Reparative Therapy of Male Homosexuality. A New Clinical Approach.* Jason Aronson Inc, 1997.

Roxburgh, Stephen. "The art of the young adult novel." *The Alan Review*, vol. 32, vol. 2, Winter 2005, pp. 4-10.

14

Silman, Anna. "8 People on Surviving Gay Conversion Therapy" *The Cut*, 10 Aug. 2018, https://www.thecut.com/2018/08/8-gay-conversion-therapy-survivors-on-cameron-post.html#comments. Accessed on August 1st, 2021.

Tozer, Erinn E., and McClanahan Mary K. „Treating the Purple Menace. Ethical Considerations of Conversion Therapy and Affirmative Alternatives." *The counseling psychologist*, vol. 27, no. 5, September 1999, pp. 722-742.

Williams, Imogen Russel. "What are YA books? Who is reading them? Which books count as Young Adult, and which as teen or New Adult is ambiguous, and their relationship is equally hard to define." *The Guardian,* 31. July 2014, https://www.theguardian.com/books/booksblog/2014/jul/31/ya-books-reads-young-adult-teen-new-adult-books. Accessed August 2nd, 2021.

Lightning Source UK Ltd.
Milton Keynes UK
UKHW010652090223
416681UK00007B/1971